PROTECT YOUR PEACE

50 Ways to Set Boundaries, Walk Away & Choose Yourself

THE FORTITUDE LIBRARY

COPYRIGHT

This book is part of The Fortitude Library™, a collection designed to support personal growth, resilience, wellbeing, and self-development.

Published by **The Fortitude Library**
New South Wales, Australia
Author: **Ameera C Lee**

First Edition
Cover Design by Ameera C Lee
Interior Design by Ameera C Lee

Disclaimer:
This book is intended for informational and inspirational purposes only and does not constitute medical, legal, psychological, or professional advice. Readers should seek appropriate professional guidance where necessary.

INTRODUCTION

You will not find peace by shrinking yourself.

You will not find peace by over-explaining, over-giving, or over-staying in places that quietly break you.

Peace is not something you wait for.

It is something you choose.

And choosing it will cost you.

It will cost you conversations you once tolerated.

It will cost you people you once loved.

It will cost you versions of yourself that were built to survive, not to thrive.

But what you gain is something far greater.

You gain clarity.

You gain self-respect.

You gain a life that finally feels like yours.

This book is not about becoming cold or cutting everyone off.

It is about becoming clear.

Clear about what you allow.

Clear about what you deserve.

Clear about when it is time to stay — and when it is time to walk away.

Because peace is not passive.

It is protected.

And the moment you start protecting it...

.... everything changes!

HOW TO USE THIS BOOK

This book is designed to be simple, honest, and actionable. Each chapter gives you:

- Truths you may need to hear
- Perspective shift to change old patterns
- A practical way to apply it
- Self-discovery questions to uncover deeper truths about yourself

You don't need to read this perfectly.
You just need to read it honestly.
Take what resonates.
Come back to what challenges you.
And most importantly — apply what you learn.
Because peace is not built through reading.
It is built through decisions.

And the truth is:
Peace is not something you find.
It is something you protect.

DEDICATION

To the version of me who kept going when it would have been easier to give up.
To the quiet strength that carried me through the days no one saw.
To every wound that shaped me, and every choice that rebuilt me.
This book exists because I refused to remain where pain left me.

To my family and friends
Thank you for loving me through every season, for your patience, your faith, and for standing beside me while I learned to find my way home to myself.

To my son
You are my greatest reason
The heart behind every dream, the purpose behind every step forward.
Everything I build, I build with you in mind.

To my coach
Thank you for believing in the strength within me long before I fully recognised it myself,
and for calling it forward when I needed it most.

And to you
the one holding these pages in your hands:

If you are weary, overwhelmed, or questioning your worth, let this be your reminder

- You are allowed to choose yourself.
- You are allowed to begin again.
- You are allowed to protect your peace.

This book is for you.

CONTENTS

CONTENTS

Choose peace over chaos,

Boundaries over Burnout,

and Never Give up on Yourself.

Ameera C Lee

1.

Stop Explaining Yourself to People Committed to Misunderstanding You

Not everyone is trying to understand you.
Some people are committed to misunderstanding you because it protects their narrative.

Over-explaining is exhausting.
It drains your energy and keeps you stuck trying to be validated by people who have already decided not to see you clearly.

The right people don't require constant explanation.
They listen. They respect. They try.

Choose peace over proving your truth.

Reflect & Reset

Where am I explaining myself more than I need to?

Who am I trying to convince?

What would choosing peace instead look like today?

2.

Say No Without Guilt

No is a complete sentence.

You don't need to justify, soften, or over-explain your boundaries just to make others comfortable.

Guilt may show up when you start saying no — not because you're wrong, but because you're doing something new.

Every time you say yes to something you don't want, you say no to yourself.

Start choosing yourself.

Reflect & Reset

I feel most drained when...

I keep over-explaining because...

If I trusted myself more, I would...

3.

Walk Away from Inconsistency

Consistency builds trust.
Inconsistency creates anxiety.

Stop trying to interpret mixed signals or hold onto potential.

People show you who they are through patterns, not words.

If it's inconsistent, it's not secure.
And you deserve security.

Reflect & Reset

Peace or proving a point?

Clarity or confusion?

Self-respect or approval?

Today, I choose:

4.

Don't Negotiate Your Worth

You don't need to convince anyone to see your value.

The moment you start negotiating your worth, you've already stepped out of your power.

The right spaces recognise you.
The wrong ones make you prove yourself.

Choose environments that meet you where you are.

Reflect & Reset

Circle what feels true right now:

Over-explaining
People-pleasing
Avoiding conflict
Seeking validation

One small shift I can make:

5.

Stop Trying to Be Understood by Everyone

Not everyone will understand you — and that's okay.

Trying to be understood by everyone leads to people-pleasing, over-explaining, and shrinking yourself.

You are not here to be palatable to everyone.

Be clear. Be real.
Let the right people resonate.

Reflect & Reset

You don't need to explain your boundaries
to people who benefit from you having none.

Where in my life am I over-explaining boundaries to people who resist them?

6.

Recognise When Respect Is Missing

Respect isn't just words, it's behaviour.

Pay attention to tone, consistency, and effort.

Someone can say they care, but if their actions dismiss, belittle, or ignore you, that's not respect.

Where respect is missing, peace cannot exist.

Reflect & Reset

One boundary I will hold this week:

One thing I will stop over-explaining:

One place I will choose peace:

7.

Protect Your Time

Your time is your life. Every "yes" is a trade.

Make sure it's worth it.

Stop giving your time to things that drain you,
distract you, or deplete you.

Protect it like it matters.
Because it does.

Reflect & Reset

Where am I not being heard, and still trying harder?

What is that costing me emotionally?

What would it look like to step back instead?

8.

Don't Stay Where You Feel Small

You were not meant to shrink to fit into spaces.

If you feel dismissed, silenced, or constantly second-guessing yourself, that environment is not aligned with you.

Growth requires space.
Peace requires safety.

Choose spaces that expand you.

Reflect & Reset

I keep giving energy to...

It leaves me feeling...

What I actually need is...

9.

Choose Clarity Over Confusion

Clarity feels calm.
Confusion feels heavy.

If you're constantly questioning
where you stand with someone,
that's information.

Stop chasing clarity
from people who create confusion.

Choose what feels grounded and clear.

Reflect & Reset

My Warning Signs That I'm Leaving My Peace:

Explaining looks like...

Proving looks like...

Pleasing looks like...

Peace looks like...

10.

Stop Giving Access to Everyone

Access to you is earned,
not automatic.

Not everyone deserves
your time,
your energy,
or your vulnerability.

Be selective.

Not everyone needs
full access to your life.

Peace comes from boundaries.

Reflect & Reset

What am I afraid will happen if I stop explaining myself?

Is that fear true? or familiar?

What feels more aligned with who I'm becoming?

11.

Trust Your Intuition

Your intuition often speaks
before your logic catches up.

If something feels off,
it usually is.

Stop overriding your inner voice
to make others comfortable.

Your intuition is there to protect
you,
not confuse you.

Reflect & Reset

Where am I shrinking to be understood?

Who am I becoming when I do that?

What version of me deserves more space?

12.

Stop Ignoring Red Flags

Red flags don't disappear—
they repeat.

Ignoring them
doesn't make them smaller.

It makes the outcome
heavier later.

What you tolerate early,
you accept long term.

Pay attention the first time.

Reflect & Reset

Silence or over-explaining?

Boundaries or burnout?

Truth or comfort?

Today, I choose:

13.

You Don't Need Closure

Closure doesn't always come from others.

Sometimes it comes from accepting that the situation was not right for you.

Waiting for someone else to explain, apologise, or change keeps you stuck.

Give yourself the closure.
Choose peace instead of answers.

Reflect & Reset

Not everyone deserves access to your reasoning.

Where have I been giving too much access?

14.

Detach from What Drains You

Not everything deserves your emotional investment.

If something consistently drains you,
it is not meant to be held onto.

Detachment is not cold - it is clarity.

Let go of what costs you your peace.

Reflect & Reset

One conversation I will stop rehearsing:

One situation I will release:

One way I will protect my energy:

15.

Choose Yourself Consistently

Choosing yourself is not a one-time decision.

It is something you practice - daily.

In your boundaries. In your decisions. In what you tolerate.

You teach people how to treat you by how you treat yourself.

Reflect & Reset

What am I trying to fix that isn't mine to fix?

Why am I holding onto it?

What would letting go feel like?

16.

Stop Overgiving

Overgiving is often rooted in the hope that you'll be valued more.

But the truth is, it often leads to being taken for granted.

Give where it's reciprocated.

Not where it's expected.

Reflect & Reset

I feel pressure to explain when...

That pressure comes from...

I can release it by...

17.

Don't Chase People

You should not have to chase connection, effort, or consistency.

What's meant for you meets you.

Chasing creates imbalance.

Peace comes from mutual effort.

Reflect & Reset

Right now I feel:

Overwhelmed / Drained / Frustrated / Clear / Grounded

What I need most is:

18.

Set Boundaries Early

Boundaries set late feel like rejection.

Boundaries set early create clarity.

You don't need to wait until you're overwhelmed to speak up.

Start early. Stay clear.

Reflect & Reset

Where am I giving explanations instead of setting boundaries?

What boundary is actually needed here?

What's one step I can take?

19.

Stop Accepting Half Effort

Half effort leads to full disappointment.

If someone only shows up when it suits them, believe that pattern.

You deserve consistency, not convenience.

Reflect & Reset

What is draining my energy? →

What truth do I need to acknowledge? →

What is my next aligned step? →

20.

Walk Away Without Drama

Not every exit needs an explanation, a speech, or closure.

Sometimes the most powerful move is quiet.

Peace doesn't require an audience.

Reflect & Reset

Who consistently makes me feel like I need to explain myself?

How does that impact my peace?

What would choosing distance look like?

21.

Don't Internalise Everything

Not everything is about you.

Sometimes people project their own issues, insecurities, or limitations.

Don't carry what isn't yours.

Reflect & Reset

You are allowed to outgrow the need to be understood by everyone.

Where am I still holding onto that need?

22.

Let People Be Who They Are

Stop trying to change people.

See them clearly, not for their potential.

Acceptance brings clarity.

Clarity brings peace.

Reflect & Reset

Holding on or letting go?

Explaining or releasing?

Chasing or choosing myself?

Today, I choose:

23.

Stop Justifying Bad Behaviour

Understanding someone's past does not excuse their behaviour.

You can have empathy without accepting mistreatment.

Reflect & Reset

Where am I staying in cycles that drain me?

What keeps me there?

What would breaking the cycle look like?

24.

Choose Environments That Feel Safe

Peace grows in safe environments.

If you feel anxious, on edge, or unsure — listen to that.

Safety is not negotiable.

Reflect & Reset

I keep repeating...

It feels like...

I'm ready to change...

25.

Don't Ignore Your Needs

Your needs matter.

Minimising them to keep others comfortable creates imbalance.

Speak them. Honour them.

Reflect & Reset

One habit I will interrupt:

One thought I will challenge:

One action I will take:

26.

Stop Tolerating Disrespect

Disrespect grows where it's tolerated.

The moment you accept it, it becomes the standard.

Raise your standard.

Reflect & Reset

What am I tolerating that no longer aligns with me?

Why have I accepted it?

What would raising my standard look like?

27.

Take Breaks Without Guilt

Rest is not weakness.

You don't need to earn your rest through exhaustion.

Pause. Reset. Protect your energy.

Reflect & Reset

I've been prioritising:

Others / Expectations / Fear / Peace / Growth

What I want to prioritise instead:

28.

Don't Engage in Every Argument

Not every situation requires your response.

Silence is sometimes the strongest boundary.

Protect your energy, not your ego.

Reflect & Reset

Growth often looks like choosing differently, not explaining more.

Where can I choose differently?

29.

Be Comfortable Being Misunderstood

Choosing yourself may not always be understood by others.

That doesn't make it wrong.

It makes it necessary.

Reflect & Reset

Realign With Your Peace

What I need to let go of →

What I need to hold onto →

What I need to move toward →

30.

Stop Overthinking Everything

Overthinking creates noise.

Peace comes from clarity, not constant analysis.

Trust yourself more.

Reflect & Reset

Where am I seeking validation instead of trusting myself?

What do I already know deep down?

What would self-trust look like today?

31.

Let Go of Control

You cannot control others — only yourself.

Trying to control outcomes leads to frustration.

Release what isn't yours to hold.

Reflect & Reset

I doubt myself when...

But the truth is...

Today I will trust...

32.

Don't Stay Out of Habit

Familiar does not mean right.

Just because something is comfortable doesn't mean it's healthy.

Choose growth over familiarity.

Reflect & Reset

Fear or faith in myself?

Hesitation or action?

Approval or self-trust?

Today, I choose:

33.

Stop Explaining Your Boundaries

Your boundaries are valid, even if others don't agree.

You don't need to convince people to respect them.

You enforce them.

Reflect & Reset

What feels heavy in my life right now?

What part of that can I release?

What would lightness feel like?

34.

Walk Away from Disrespectful Communication

Tone matters.

If someone speaks to you with disrespect, dismissiveness, or aggression — that's your signal.

You don't have to stay.

Reflect & Reset

One thing I will stop carrying:

One thing I will start doing:

One thing I will remind myself:

35.

Choose Peace Over Winning

Winning an argument doesn't always mean you win peace.

Sometimes the strongest move is stepping back.

Peace is the priority.

Reflect & Reset

Peace is not found in explaining — it's found in choosing.

Where do I need to choose differently?

36.

Don't Ignore Patterns

One incident can be a mistake.

Repeated behaviour is a pattern.

Pay attention to patterns.

Reflect & Reset

Where am I holding onto something out of habit, not alignment?

What would alignment look like instead?

What's one shift I can make today?

37.

Be Selective with Your Energy

Your energy is limited.

Be intentional about where you invest it.

Not everything deserves your attention.

Reflect & Reset

Peace Reset

The habit I need to notice →

The truth I need to acknowledge →

The change I need to make →

38.

Stop Seeking External Validation

You don't need constant approval to feel secure.

Build internal validation.

That's where peace lives.

Reflect & Reset

Today I feel:

Calm / Tired / Overwhelmed / Focused / Disconnected

What I need right now:

39.

Walk Away from Emotional Chaos

Peace and chaos cannot coexist.

If something constantly feels overwhelming, unstable, or draining — Step back.

Choose calm.

Reflect & Reset

I keep going back to...

Even though it makes me feel...

I deserve to feel...

40.

Don't Accept Breadcrumbs

Minimal effort is not enough.

You deserve consistency, effort, and intention.

Anything less creates imbalance.

Reflect & Reset

Where am I abandoning myself to keep the peace?

What is that costing me?

What would choosing myself look like?

41.

Speak Up When Something Feels Off

Silence can cost you your peace.

If something doesn't feel right, address it early.

Clarity protects you.

Reflect & Reset

Keeping the peace or keeping myself?

Silence or self-respect?

Comfort or growth?

Today, I choose:

42.

Stop Repeating the Same Cycles

If you keep ending up in the same situation, pause and reflect.

Patterns don't change without awareness.

Choose differently.

Reflect & Reset

You don't lose people by choosing yourself.

You lose what was never aligned.

Where does this resonate?

43.

Don't Confuse Potential with Reality

Potential is not reality.

Don't stay based on what something could be.

Stay based on what it is.

Reflect & Reset

One place I will speak up:

One place I will step back:

One way I will honour myself:

44.

Let Go Without Closure

Sometimes there is no final conversation.

No explanation. No apology.

Peace comes from acceptance.

Reflect & Reset

What am I holding onto that is already letting go of me?

Why is it hard to release?

What would freedom feel like?

45.

Choose Yourself in Difficult Moments

Choosing yourself is not always easy.

It may feel uncomfortable at first.

But discomfort leads to growth.

And growth leads to peace.

Reflect & Reset

Peace Reset

What I am still holding on to →

What I am ready to release →

My next aligned step →

46.

Don't Stay Where You're Not Valued

You should not have to earn basic respect and appreciation.

If you feel overlooked, undervalued, or invisible — leave.

You deserve more.

Reflect & Reset

I've been telling myself...

But a more supportive truth is...

I choose to believe...

47.

Stop Giving Second Chances Without Change

Second chances without change lead to repeated outcomes.

Accountability matters.

Watch actions, not words.

Reflect & Reset

Right now I am:

Overthinking / Avoiding / Growing / Healing / Learning

What this moment is teaching me:

48.

Protect Your Emotional Energy

Not everything deserves your emotional response.

Learn when to step back, detach, and protect your state.

Peace requires boundaries.

Reflect & Reset

What version of me am I stepping into?

What do I need to leave behind?

What does this next chapter require of me?

49.

Accept When It's Time to Move On

Holding on doesn't always mean strength.

Sometimes it means resistance.

Letting go creates space for better.

Reflect & Reset

Choosing peace is not weakness — it is power.

Where can I step into that power?

50.

Build a Life That Feels Peaceful

Peace is not something you wait for.

It's something you build — through your choices, your boundaries, and your standards.

Choose what feels right.
Choose what feels calm.
Choose what feels aligned.
Choose yourself.

Reflect & Reset

What have I learned about myself through this journey?

What am I no longer willing to tolerate?

What am I choosing moving forward?

Congratulations

You made it here.
That may not seem like much to anyone else— but it matters.
Because choosing peace is not easy. It means walking away when it would be easier to stay.
It means saying no when you are used to saying yes.
It means disappointing others so you stop abandoning yourself.
And you did that.
Even reading this book is a decision, a decision to grow, to reflect.
To stop repeating what hurts you. To choose a different way forward. That takes strength. But this is not the finish line.
Peace is not something you choose once-it is something you practice.
In the boundaries you hold. In the standards you keep.
In the conversations you walk away from.
In the patterns you refuse to repeat.
Some days you will do this well, some days you will forget.
Some days you will slip back into old habits, because healing is not linear. What matters is that you keep returning to yourself.
Keep choosing what protects your peace.
Keep choosing what honours your growth.
Keep choosing what aligns with who you are becoming.
And when it gets hard - read these pages again.
You deserve peace. You deserve respect.
You deserve the life that comes when you stop betraying yourself to keep others comfortable.

Keep going. This is only the beginning.

ABOUT THE AUTHOR

Ameera C. Lee is an author, speaker, Paralympian, and advocate for mental wellbeing, resilience, and personal growth.

Balancing life as a full-time professional, mother and athlete, she brings a grounded, real-world perspective shaped by discipline, adversity, and lived experience.

Through her writing, she helps individuals navigate challenges, rebuild self-worth, and create lives rooted in strength, clarity, self-respect and authenticity.

Her work is honest, practical, and empowering. Designed to help people choose themselves, set boundaries, and move forward with confidence.

She doesn't just write about resilience — she lives it.

The Fortitude Library

Your Journey Continues

If this book resonated with you, this is just the beginning. Explore more from The Fortitude Library — a collection of books designed to strengthen your mindset, support your wellbeing, and help you build a life you're proud of.

Upcoming in the series:

- Keep Going Anyway
- The Resilient Mind (Colouring Book)
- The Fortitude Library Puzzle Book (Core mind and focus)

THE FORTITUDE LIBRARY

Made in the USA
Middletown, DE
05 November 2026

36545552R10071